Also by DJ Geribo

The House at the Top of the Trees

Eddie Easel and the Case of the Missing Green

The Miracle Dog

Mouse Bound

Seven Storied Houses

All titles available from BBD Publishing at www.BBDPublishing.com
or from the author's website at www.DJGeribo.com

Selected titles available on Amazon in softbound and e-book formats.

ME
&
THEM

ME
&
THEM

Memories of Mom and Dad

DJ Geribo

bd

BBD Publishing ~ Alton, NH

Me & Them is published by

> BBD Publishing
> P.O. Box 351
> Alton, NH 03809

www.BBDPublishing.com

Book Layout and Book Design by DJ Geribo and James J. Fontaine
Book Editing by James J. Fontaine

Cover Design by Positively Creative Solutions, LLC

Photos Copyright by the Individuals as Credited

Printed in the United States of America

10 9 8 7 6 5 4 3 2 1

Library of Congress Control Number: 2021950076

ISBN 978-0-9883068-6-8

Dedicated to my parents:

Vincent S. Geribo and Thelma M. Geribo

TABLE OF CONTENTS

Preface

The stories in this collection are taken, mostly, from my childhood and represent what life was like in a working-class family in the 1950's. Or more specifically, in our family. Although many of them are based on true incidents that happened in my life, several of them are helped with the creativity of fiction added in, mostly because I can't remember exactly everything that happened in day-to-day life when I was a child. But, also because that is how many writers of fiction write their stories; based on true life with a little fiction spread throughout.

Some might ask whether the title is, well, "a bit impersonal, don't you think?" The "Them" I am referring to, after all, are my parents. That is how we sometimes talk about a couple of people, as 'them' or 'they'. I guess I could have said, 'my parents and me', but it sounded too proper for the kinds of stories I was sharing. And I would not agree with the idea that I was being too impersonal because how much do we really know about our parents? Unless they sit you down and tell you the story of their lives, you mostly have to fill in a lot of blanks. So, they are kind of like strangers to you. How much do we really know anyone?

But our parents, I believe, we know least of all. Particularly if you were born in the 1950's when people never talked about their lives. They just kept all the pain and abuse they may have suffered inside. No one wanted to talk about it. Maybe they didn't care or maybe it was too embarrassing and uncomfortable to listen to – how can someone tolerate such abuse? And no one knew anything about self-help or read anything about healing your inner child – those books weren't around at that time. So how do you fix it when you are no longer in that situation and you are now an adult? Also, people who lived through the Great Depression and World War II had their own problems to deal with, the least of which was the lack of so many things.

For my parents, I have no doubt my mom was in an abusive situation when she was a child. My mom was the second eldest of six siblings, 3 girls and 3 boys, with an older half-brother. Her mother also had several miscarriages. My dad, I think, was just lost in the middle of a family with eight children. No college degrees among any of them; my dad was a blue-collar working man, my mom a farm girl. The military brought them together. And then dad brought mom back to Massachusetts where his brothers and sisters lived with their families. This is where they remained, raising three kids.

Surprising to me sometimes is how the three of us came out without too many permanent scars; I've often referred to my parents as two people who knew nothing about everything. But for all the mistakes they both made along the way, I believe they each did the best they could with what they knew.

DJ Geribo
November, 2021

Mom

Me & Them

From Country Girl to City Girl

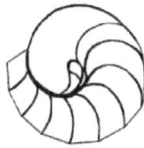

Marrying my dad and moving to an east coast city must have been an almost unimaginable change, combined with culture shock, for a country girl like my mom. She spent her life until early adulthood in Kansas when her family then moved to Utah. Not a major change, I imagine – still lots of dirt roads, still dirt poor. But then, my mom never felt she deserved anything and as the second oldest of six, there was no end to the lack they must have endured on a daily basis. How do I know this? Because I suffer from the same condition. Yes, the 'lack' gene was passed down to me.

But I wonder if what she shared with my dad – an apartment, never a house, three kids, couches with burn holes from the times dad fell asleep smoking when he came home from the barroom drunk – lived up to whatever expectations she might have had for herself? Or did she have any expectations at all? Was almost anything better than the poverty she experienced as a young girl? Did she even consider herself poor when she was growing up since most likely all of her neighbors lived similar lives of lack?

I do remember one story my mom shared about when she and her siblings went to church, shoeless. As children often think when they become aware of others, she was sure everyone was looking at her bare feet and became, in that instant, self-conscious and embarrassed. Perhaps even in that moment she became aware of the poverty her family endured since everyone else in church, or so it appeared to a child, wore shoes except she and her siblings.

As an adult, my mom appeared to have a shoe fetish that rivaled Imelda Marcos'. But I know she was just making up for the lack and embarrassment she experienced as that shoeless child.

Me & Them

Highfalutin Ideas

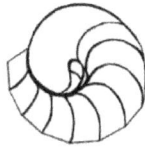

My mom never finished high school. Which was probably just one of the reasons why her self-esteem was so obviously low. Growing up on a farm in Kansas back in the 1920's and 30's certainly made it difficult to get an education at all. But to finish high school was nearly impossible. As the oldest girl in her family, she needed to get a job and make some money to help support the family. But according to stories my mom told, she loved learning. She would come home from school and share with her mom what she had learned that day. Typically, moms support their children and you would hope that her mom would have done the right thing. But she didn't. Her mom, instead, shamed her oldest daughter by accusing her of having 'highfalutin' ideas.

I looked up 'highfalutin' to find a similar word that was a little more modern and relatable. The word the dictionary gave was 'pretentious' which means, 'attempting to impress by affecting greater importance, talent, culture, etc., than is actually possessed.' I interpret what her mom was saying to her oldest daughter was, 'Who do you think you are? How dare you try to rise above the position you've been dealt in this life. Get back down here with the rest of us hard-working farmers and don't try to better yourself.' Now, I'm not saying anything at all negative about farmers, what I'm saying is, she didn't want her daughter to be anyone other than what she was herself: someone who had to work hard for a living. Grandma, unlike my mom, was pregnant at 15. But, that's another story.

I'm proud to have inherited my mom's highfalutin ideas. Not only did I graduate from high school, but I also went on to receive my Bachelor of Arts in English and certification as a programmer. And now, even to this day, I never stop learning. Thanks, mom, for passing on to me your 'highfalutin' ideas.

Me & Them

Doctors, Dentists, and
Other Unnecessary Professions

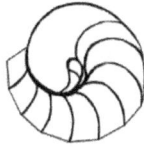

We had a family doctor, the same doctor so many other people who grew up in the 1950's had, and that was Dr. Mom. My mom always seemed to know what to do to take care of us. We all had the flu, we all had the measles, we all had the mumps, and we all had regular seasonal colds. Only my brother had scarlatina – he was quarantined in his bedroom – and that was the only time my mom called a doctor who came to our home. It turns out it was the milder form of scarlet fever; but you wouldn't know it with my brother who, no matter what illness he had, was always in more pain than anyone else in the family. (My brother always was a drama queen!)

When I was about 3 or 4 years old, I accidently spilled boiling water onto myself that my mom had just poured into a teacup for herself and I was brought to a doctor. I was fortunate that I never had any scars as a result of this incident. But, other than the one doctor's visit for my brother and the visits I made to the doctor to remove the dead skin from my arm as the new skin grew in underneath, we never had another real doctor tend to any of us. My parents also tended to themselves when most people would have consulted a doctor. Of course, my mom did have a doctor when she had each of her children. But, other than that, she also avoided any doctor visits. I think it was mostly because when my dad was a tailor, they had no health insurance.

I do remember going to a dentist when I was in elementary school. The public school provided a service to children and periodically we went for check-ups or to have our teeth pulled or a cavity filled. I will be forever grateful for the dentist who removed an eye tooth that needed to come out to allow my adult tooth to come in.

My mom had teeth from the mid-west. No cavities. She had her first filling when she was in her 40's; just the one, that was all she ever had! And she had her wisdom teeth removed. That's it.

My dad was not so lucky. He grew up in the Boston, MA area. Once he was out of the military, he said good-bye to doctors and dentists. For dental work my dad depended on Dr. Dad. That's right, he pulled his own teeth! A tooth would abscess, swelling his face up and contorting it into something you'd see in a late-night TV horror movie. There were these little poultice sacks you could put on a bad tooth to help relieve pain, supposedly, until you could get to the dentist. But, since the trip to the dentist never happened, I imagine the tooth simply rotted in his mouth. At least until he could pull it.

Me & Them

Mom's Mom

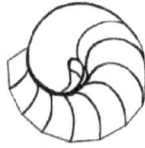

One day our neighbor from the apartment upstairs knocked on our door. They had an emergency phone call for my mom. In the 1950's we didn't have our own phone. After my mom took the call she came downstairs crying and told us that her mom had died. My parents couldn't afford for her to take a trip back to Utah.

About four years before that day, we had taken a trip to Utah by train to visit mom's parents and a couple of her siblings. My dad stayed home and worked. Although the trip was one of the most memorable times of my life, the visit to Grandma and Grandpa's tiny home was the least memorable. They lived in a converted garage with three rooms barely big enough for the two of them. We stayed with mom's sister who lived close by.

A short, round, plain woman with doughy cheeks, I was terrified of the gray-haired grandma who didn't resemble my mom at all. My mom had high cheek bones, dark hair, and with her splash of red lipstick she looked like a beauty queen to me.

Grandma collected dog figurines that sat on the shelves in her living room. I still have the one I was given; a couple of its legs broke over the years but my dad glued it back together. Grandma also made pickles, a personal favorite of mine. During our visit I really wanted one and asked my mom if I could have one and she said, "If you want one, ask your grandma." I didn't want one that bad. Grandpa, sitting in his chair in the living room most of the day, didn't have much to say.

Before visiting two of mom's other siblings, who lived in Nevada and Idaho, we took photos. A neighbor's boy sat on grandma's lap as we all posed next to the parents who were responsible for so much sadness in my mom's life.

Dad's parents were both dead before I was born. I know almost as much about them as I know about my dad.

Me & Them

Free to Drive

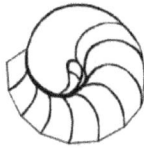

In most families, particularly in the 1950's, men did the driving. Women were housewives and stayed home and took care of the kids and the house; meaning house cleaning, ironing, cooking meals, and other domestic chores. A lot of women never learned to drive at all, depending completely on the men to drive them wherever they needed to go. Also, most households only had one car.

Not in my family. My mom did all of the driving. My dad never drove – he was the passenger in the car. I never knew why he didn't drive and I didn't really think about it as a kid but that was just the way it was in my family. Perhaps, looking back, one of the reasons was because my dad was a drinker and it was easier for him to walk everywhere or take the subway home than it was to get behind the wheel of a car and drive after he'd had too much to drink.

But I'm sure there was a reason my mom learned to drive. I think the reason had something to do with freedom. I believe she felt that if she had a car, she could take off whenever she wanted. She could go for a drive or she could get out of the house and visit family and friends. She could escape a life that maybe wasn't quite the one she pictured for herself.

Later in her life, after my dad passed away, she used this skill that she had learned so many years before and drove herself across the country, from the east coast to Utah to visit her sisters and brothers. It was that trip that brought her back to the west that she had always loved and longed for and to which she decided to return to for the rest of her life.

Me & Them

Best Friend

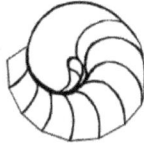

To try to make me feel more comfortable about being tall when I was a child, my mom told me about her and her best friend when she was a child. Everyone called them 'Mutt and Jeff', where my mom was Mutt, the taller one, and Jeff was her shorter friend. I often wondered, even as a child, just how short her short friend was since my mom topped out at about 5'2". I grew to 5'10".

That was back in the 1930's when my mom and her family lived in Kansas. When my siblings and I were growing up, my mom met a neighbor who lived next door to my dad's sister. Dad's sister and her family eventually moved, but they lived there long enough for my mom to become friends with the neighbor. Even though this new friend, Mary, was at least ten years older than my mom and dad and their youngest child was several years older than my oldest sister, they seemed to bond over coffee, biscuits, and conversation.

Back in the 1950's, people didn't call each other to ask if they could come for a visit, they just dropped by and chances were someone would be home. Mostly they went out to shop at the corner store so would return home soon. But typically, Mary was at home because with five children she had a lot to do while her youngest kids were at school. We would take a ride to

Mary's home on the weekends since we all went to school and that was the time when we were all available to go for a visit. Since Mary was older, a couple of her children were already out of high school and working when we met the family. Several times we would drop by after having dinner in their local downtown and before we went to the drive-in movies since they lived close to the drive-in. Other times we would be left at the house with the older kids while the parents went out to dinner.

Occasionally my mom would take me for a drive to visit Mary and they would chat while I explored outside or played with the kids in their neighborhood. For many years there were marshes behind their home. Then several years later someone bought the land and put in a driving range filling in the marshes. Many of the golf balls ended up in Mary's yard where my brother was happy to retrieve and collect them for himself.

This is also where we got our first dog, Mickey. A family who lived down the street from Mary's house was happy to have one less puppy mouth to feed and let us choose the one we wanted. She was a fox terrier mix that we took home and had for many years until she passed away.

After many years and so many visits it was a sad day for my mom when Mary passed away. Of course, all of us were married and had moved out of the house by then. But I know my mom would always miss the woman who had become, almost by accident, her best friend.

I'm pretty sure dad didn't have a best friend. Unless you count the man who came to his funeral.

Me & Them

Christmas Cards

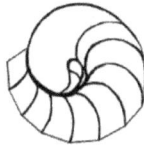

In the 1950's and 60's, sending Christmas cards was as much a part of Christmas as putting up a tree and buying and wrapping presents. Hearing from family and friends across the country was almost a miracle to some; especially people who lived as rurally as my mom did when she was growing up. But sending Christmas cards to loved ones was a strong tradition in our home as it was with so many families we knew. In the month before Christmas and just after Thanksgiving we had mail delivered twice a day since the post office was inundated with so many cards. It was always exciting to see who sent the cards, in what part of the country they lived, and what was going on in their lives. We didn't have a telephone and so this was often the only time my mom heard from many people from her past.

For so many years Christmas cards represented a way for people who lived far away from each other to connect once a year. It was a task my mom took on alone every year. Even though it seemed to take her weeks to complete, I think she looked forward to it. For the majority of cards she filled out, she simply signed our names and filled out the addresses on the envelope. But for her family and friends out west, a letter always accompanied the card. Writing these letters would take mom several days and often brought out the tears as she thought about how much she missed her family and friends on the other side of the country.

We hung the cards we received around the living room, happy to show off the uniquely individual cards sent by so many people. It was a tradition we all enjoyed and one we all continued after we left home. And then as the years went by and some of the relatives died, the number of cards we received dwindled. We no longer received cards twice a day in the mail. My mom no longer had to buy two boxes, or more, of 50 cards each. And each year we seemed to receive fewer and fewer cards.

Sending Christmas cards is one of those traditions that lived on for years, decades. It seems we have so few traditions left that have been passed down. And now many people only send e-cards for Christmas and birthdays. Although the world, with the internet, has become a smaller place, I can't hold an e-card in my hand, or save it in a box with all of my other beloved Christmas cards. I still have the picture postcard of my mom that she sent to her parents at Christmas in the 1930's that I can hold and look at whenever I want. I marvel at the thought that it is around 90 years old! Those e-cards that people sent to me have most likely been deleted.

Me & Them

Green Stamps

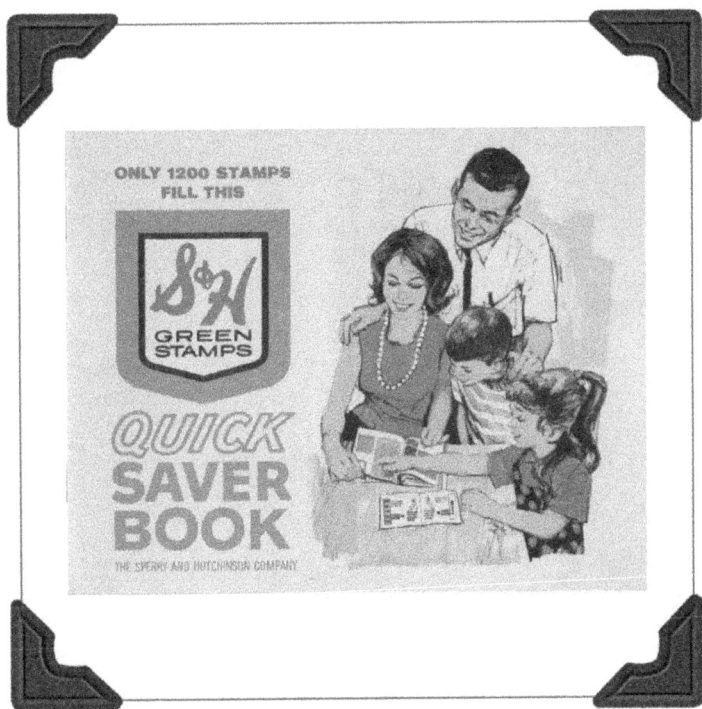

ONLY 1200 STAMPS
FILL THIS

S&H
GREEN
STAMPS

QUICK
SAVER
BOOK

THE SPERRY AND HUTCHINSON COMPANY

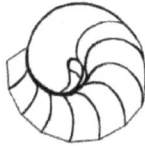

I remember during the 1950's when the supermarkets gave out Green Stamps with your food order. The amount of money you spent determined how many stamps you would get. Each week my mom would come home with sheets of Green Stamps that we would 'lick and stick' into small booklets.

The booklets contained about 20 4"x6" pages and when they were filled you could purchase any number of items from the Green Stamp catalogs. The Green Stamps were like money and considered valuable to a working-class family of five. One item I remember my mom buying with the stamps was an olive-green hassock. It felt like we were getting home furnishings for free.

I don't know what happened to the Green Stamps or why they went away. But I have memories of my mom pasting the stamps into the little booklets. It was a chore worthy of her time since she would plan for the next item she wanted to 'purchase'. And since she was shopping at the supermarket anyway, the Green Stamps really were a bonus.

There were other 'free' type items that my mom got over the years. Glasses used to come in a box of laundry detergent. And she and my sister would go to an event where my mom would win another piece of china. I don't think she ever got the entire set of plates, cups, and saucers. But I do still have the blue platter that she won so many years ago.

Me & Them

Perms

JUL   ·   58

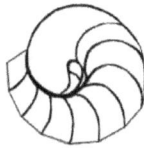

During the 1950's what mother didn't want her little girl to look like Shirley Temple? The darling of Hollywood and a superstar at the young age of 3, she danced her way into America's heart. But those curls, which her mother pinned up for every movie, were Shirley's crowning glory. And mothers around the country tried to duplicate the look for their own daughters, often giving their girls a home permanent, which came out in 1944. I know my mom did.

My mom was an advocate of the home perm not only for me but for herself, as well. I recently looked at a black-and-white photo of my mom when she was in grammar school and saw a girl with dark hair that looked like a bowl had been put on her head and a cut made with scissors around the shape of the bowl, which, I was told, many people did when it was time to cut their children's hair. But my mom loved curly hair. I, too, loved curly hair and for many years I also permed my hair. Until I didn't and discovered that I had naturally wavy hair, which I got from my dad.

Some of my mom's perms had been OK. Some had been way over-processed. At least she never lost any hair, but I can't be positive about that. My sister wasn't as lucky and one time, when she was in her late teens, she permed her hair too close to the time she colored it and she was horrified, as my mom rinsed her hair, watching the pieces break off until her hair was about an inch long. My mom did color (always a reddish color) and perm her own hair, but I'm pretty sure she never experienced breakage like that. Later on, perms were greatly improved and not as damaging to hair.

But curly hair was what my mom always wanted. And she continued to perm her hair right up until her cancer treatments when her hair fell out. As it grew back in, she was amazed that it was growing back a dark brown color, which was her original color, just like in her black-and-white school girl photo.

Me & Them

The Lipstick

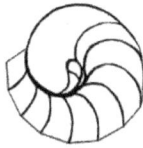

She picked the tube up off her mother's bureau. There was only one. It was shorter than a crayon but fatter. The gold metal case was shiny. There was a label on the bottom, round like the tube, that read Max Factor and, in even smaller print, the words Bold Red.

The cover was tight but she pulled it off and carefully placed it on the bureau. She had seen her mother do it so many times before; with one hand she held the tube while she turned the bottom with her other hand. A Bold Red pillar surfaced, and with it the sweet, rich, aroma that meant dressing up in a black silk sheath with matching high heels, going out to a night club, sipping a highball and leaving a bold kiss on the rim of the cocktail glass.

Not until years later could she understand that the lipstick allowed her mother entrance to a place far from the apartment with worn linoleum floors and wallpaper that was peeling in places and dirty around the light switches. In this other world she imagined her mother could be anyone else, a woman alone waiting for her date who would appear in a limo to take her to dinner at an all-night bistro. Or they could go back to the mansion they shared in Beverly Hills. The possibilities were unlimited.

But then, the tube retracted, the cover was replaced, and the illusion ended.

Me & Them

Hiding Behind a Smile

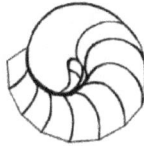

One of the most obvious flaws about my mom was her teeth. She would never smile and show her teeth or when she laughed loudly, her hand always covered her mouth to hide her two front teeth that stuck out. She was kind of vague about what happened, but her front teeth, somehow, had been knocked out when she was a child and as they grew back in, she told us she kept putting her tongue in the space so that the teeth grew in sticking out. She couldn't afford to have braces so lived with teeth that caused her endless embarrassment.

Her hand, a drink, or a smile instead of a laugh, these were the props mom used to hide her teeth. It became such a normal response she didn't have to think twice about it. This was a life-long affliction that lived on in my mom's mouth. Even her wedding photo shows a woman smiling with her mouth closed. She certainly would not want anyone to see the two front teeth that had caused her so much pain over the years.

Many years later my mom, while living in Utah after my dad had died, got her front teeth replaced. She was so happy to finally have teeth she could show off and not try to hide. She even sent me a photo of her smiling big with her new straight front teeth. I was so happy she could finally smile and laugh without feeling self-conscious. She was able, finally, to rid herself of one of her many insecurities.

Me & Them

Favorite Foods

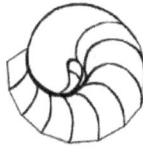

My mom was a good cook. I don't know if she was when my dad first met her, but if I had to guess I would say that she knew more than a lot of women since she was the second oldest of six and most likely was doing a lot of cooking from an early age. I remember she told me how her mom liked to work in the fields with the men so, since mom was the oldest girl, she had to tend to her younger siblings and take care of the house. But there were definitely recipes she learned over the years that added to the many that she already knew how to make.

Not a gourmet cook, most of the recipes mom made were hearty dishes that could be stretched out for many meals. I have no doubt she learned this way of cooking when she was young since there were so many mouths to feed – at least 8 at any one time. With our family, meals could last for several days and could turn into other meals just by adding a few different ingredients. For example, a turkey would feed us all for several dinners and sandwiches for lunch. Then some of the turkey would end up in a casserole with noodles and cream of mushroom soup. And then finally, the rest of the turkey including the carcass would be thrown into a stock pot with water, carrots, celery, and barley for a soup that we would have for several more days. A turkey was definitely an economical choice when looking for something that would last for many meals to feed a family of five.

I have many food memories from my childhood. To please my dad, my mom learned to cook a few traditional Lithuanian dishes from my dad's older sister. Although my dad's palate was not very sophisticated, since he was a smoker and a drinker, he did enjoy the dishes that he grew up eating in his boyhood home. There were many times when I walked in the door coming home from school and was greeted by the smell of home-made bread – and this was all made by hand since there were no bread machines back then or if there were, they certainly were not on my mom's 'must have' list. But the warm bread aroma was comforting like a cup of hot chocolate on a winter's day, which was usually when mom made bread. Another wonderful smell was mom's home-made spaghetti sauce, a recipe she got from an Italian neighbor of one of my aunts. I, fortunately, got this recipe and, to this day, still make it the same way and I still love it.

Although I no longer eat meats other than turkey, the smell of beef stew, another specialty of mom's, made my stomach growl when I walked in the door and smelled the beef, vegetables, and dumplings bubbling in the pot. Dumplings, although made simply of Bisquick mix and water, was what I liked best about the beef stew.

The smells from the Lithuanian dishes my mom made were a little less appetizing. One in particular, caboosta soup (surely not the correct spelling for the soup but the one I've used my entire life), hit you like a slap across the face with a dish cloth that had been soaking in swill and sitting in the compost for a few weeks! A poor man's soup, its main ingredients were shredded cabbage, sauerkraut, and salt and pepper. To dress up the soup and give it a little protein, country-style spare ribs were added to the soup. The ribs did nothing to improve the smell.

Made with some of the most unusual ingredients, Lithuanian dishes were typically comprised of simple and few ingredients. One meal I enjoy and try to make at least once every year is something called klatskis – another dish mom learned from dad's oldest sister. A meat ball inside a dumpling made of dough, these are boiled in a pot of water with pieces of salt pork for about ½ hour and eaten with sour cream. (I use ground turkey and have even tried it using veggie meat balls, and use veggie bacon instead of salt pork.) And then there is koshalina. One ingredient I know for sure is pig's feet. When all the ingredients were cooked together in a pot, they were then poured into a glass baking dish and chilled on the back porch in the winter months. When it finished setting, it was then sliced and eaten. I know it was a dish my dad liked but I have memories of her making it only a couple of times.

I have the least pleasant memories of my mom trying to teach me how to make a pie crust. Hers was the best, still is in my opinion, although my sister's is pretty close to mom's crust. Mom tried to show me, working the dough, always getting her hands right in there. In my 20's and newly married and also not as interested in baking as I was in cooking, I obviously wasn't doing it right and she quickly pushed me out of the way and finished making the dough for the pie crust. I stood by, watching, not offering to help. And now, so many years later, I truly wish I had paid more attention to her pie crust making expertise.

I do occasionally cook as my mom did, preferring to make a meal that we can have for several days so I don't have to think about cooking every day; things like turkeys, casseroles, and soups, even though there has only been two of us to cook for in my own home. But I treasure these few recipes I got from my mom and hope my siblings have passed them down to their children.

Me & Them

The Pants in the Family

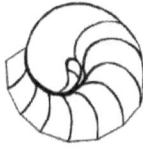

In most families, when a child did something wrong that needed to be punished the threat was 'wait until your father gets home.' But not in our house. We never feared dad coming home from work to discipline us. It just never happened. The one to fear was mom. She was the one who made the rules, who dished out the discipline, the praise, and the chores. Basically, mom made all the decisions in the family. Dad was often more like one of the kids and his lack of involvement was unique among dads. But I think that was typical in the 1950's – a lot of dads just weren't as involved in family life as they seem to be now; but they were the disciplinarians. Just not in our family.

Mom was tough. As the second oldest in a family of 6 living a hard farm life, there really wasn't any other way for her to be. So yes, she was the one to fear.

But, while she was tough on the outside, she was soft, insecure, and lacking in confidence on the inside. I remember hearing mom say, more than once, that she did not want this role but my dad wasn't interested in it and someone had to 'wear the pants' so she put them on. Mom was used to the 'man of the house' being the boss and the dad. I doubt if she realized, when she married my dad, that she would be taking on that role.

Me & Them

Westerns

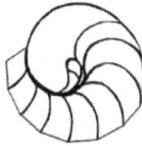

My mom could curl up with a good western TV series the way most people curl up with a good book. In the 1950's and 60's there were a lot of western shows on, not only weekly TV series but movies, also. Some of her favorites were Bonanza, Cheyenne, Laramie, Wagon Train, and the Rifleman. She also occasionally read a western by Zane Grey. She was an avid reader but mostly of romance-type novels. I read one, once. They are not my thing, nor are westerns – although, truth be told, I've never read one.

Westerns have experienced a resurgence recently but they aren't as popular as they once were. I sometimes see a movie on the Hallmark Channel where the story takes place on a ranch. "Dallas" was on in the late 70's. And there was a movie called "Unforgiven" with Clint Eastwood in 1992 and a couple of series like "The Son" and "Yellowstone" just a couple of years back. Even today there are a few like "Longmire" that have caught some interest. Maybe people are looking for a simpler time since our lives have become so busy and complex. But westerns typically come and go, not hanging around very long. The wild west just doesn't seem to have the appeal it once did.

My mom was hooked on westerns because she grew up in the west; Kansas and Utah. She had a hard life working on a farm and left home to get a job in a hotel; it was run by the mother of a family she grew up with in Utah. She always romanticized the 'old west' and wanted to go back there. My dad grew up near the city of Boston and that was where mom and dad settled. We lived driving distance from his brothers, sisters, and their families. So, she learned to adapt to city life and focused on her children as each one came along.

After my dad passed, my mom returned to her roots and reconnected with her first boyfriend, the son of the woman who ran the hotel where she had lived and worked. Maybe all along that was what she missed about the west.

Me & Them

The Flying Shoe

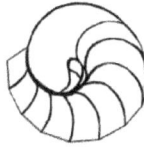

To say my mom was reactionary would be putting it mildly. She could fly off the handle, pick something up, and send it rocketing your way before you had a chance to turn out of the path of the shoe, brush, or any other readily available object that was close at hand, there to do the deed. And the deed was, to stop you in your tracks and get back at you for some unkind or sarcastic words you just said to her.

I remember seeing Eddie Murphy when he was in his prime doing standup comedy. He did a skit talking about the flying shoe. His mother and my mom apparently attended the same school of child discipline for whatever the crime might be. I don't think I ever connected so strongly with a comedian.

But we became quite adept at avoiding the shoe rocketing towards us. It was like a hit and run; we said something nasty then got up from the chair where we were sitting and dashed out of the living room and down the hallway. Just like Eddie Murphy's mom, we knew she could curve that shoe so that it flew through the doorway, took a left and followed us as we ran. We had to be fast, really fast. Sometimes we made it but sometimes mom was so much faster. I mean, she had to bend down and grab the shoe from the floor, pull her throwing arm back, and let it go before we got out of the room. All we had to do was get up off the chair and run.

This was definitely one of my mom's trademark moves. Swearing was one of the other ways she expressed her anger. Not the F-bomb, never the F-bomb. But 'you son-of-a-bitch' usually accompanied the flying shoe.

Me & Them

The Photo Drawer

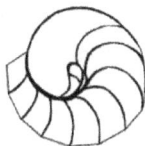

Most people use their bureaus to store their clothes. You have an underwear drawer, maybe one for sweaters. Another might be for pajamas or t-shirts. And most people probably have a sock drawer. My parents had a photograph drawer. Or I should say, my mom had a photograph drawer since at least 99% of the photos in the drawer were hers. And we couldn't get enough of them.

Every Thanksgiving we would open that drawer and out would come the photos, spread all over my parents' bed. Who's this, mom? Oh, that was my Aunt Alta. And who is the dog sitting at the piano? That was Aunt Alta's dog, Mickey. (Our dog, who started out as Wiggles, would come to inherit that name not long after we got her because she reminded my mom of Aunt Alta's dog.) And who are these guys? Those are my brothers, your uncles, Ed and Newman. And that one is Claude. And this is Aunt Joetta and Edith with me when we were all married and the men in the photo are our husbands, uncle Leon, uncle Jack, and your dad. I could almost hear my mom sigh and sometimes I knew she was holding back tears.

Over the years mom started to forget some of the people in the photos. They might have been distant relatives or friends of the family. I don't have any of those photos. My sister might have some. But it didn't really make sense for us to keep those photos since they usually weren't directly related to us or were so far removed that they held no lasting memory for us. Or they had all been dead for so long that my mom no longer remembered who any of them were. She did sometimes refer to someone as 'I think that is a second cousin.' or 'Oh, she was our neighbor when I lived in Kansas.'

It is sad to think about the photo drawer's demise. After we moved from that apartment, we never really looked at the photos anymore. I'm not even sure where my mom put them. I think my sister got most of them, and maybe my brother took a few, so they could pass them down to their children. But I think there were a lot of photos that just didn't make it. After my dad passed and she left the state heading out west and back to her roots, the truck that carried her furniture and belongings caught on fire and she lost many things. Some of the damage was to her photos. I hope it was only the ones of the people she could no longer identify.

Me & Them

Latch Key Kid

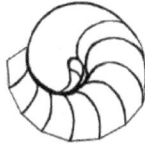

Several years ago, I remember hearing a term that I found to be both humorous and a bit outdated although the reference was that it was a new term, something just invented. The term 'latchkey kid' was in the news and people were talking about the middle-school-aged kids coming home from school to empty homes with both parents at work.

I grew up in the 1950's and 60's when the majority of women were housewives and at home when their pre-teens and younger children got home from school. Mom was always there to greet them, often providing them with a snack of cookies and milk. Yes, the "Leave it to Beaver" scenario was alive and well in middle America.

Not in my house. Through much of my childhood, from elementary grades on, my mom worked. Since she did not have a high school education her jobs were all service or factory-related. One job was in a laundromat where people would drop off their clothes. My mom would launder and fold the dried clothes, ready for people to pick up. And then she had another job working for a company that made Common Crackers. Considered New England's classic cracker, they have been around since the 1800's. No one knows for sure who created the

Common Cracker but many New England states made them. I don't know what her job was there, but again most likely it was some kind of manual labor position.

When I started high school, we moved to North Quincy, MA. My mom got a job at a department store called The Bargain Center. She worked there for many years, even becoming manager of the children's department. She left that job when my dad got really sick from cancer and she needed to take care of him so she retired after that.

Me & Them

Habitual

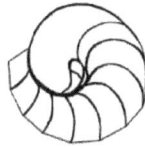

We all have habits, some good some bad. Some are just annoying, particularly if they are habits of other people. Some people's habits are more self-destructive like biting their nails or pulling out their hair. Or some just quietly blink, again and again, whether or not they really need to blink. Of course, there are the habits that are actually disorders like the obsessive-compulsive ones where a person has to touch the door knob 10 or 20 times before leaving their house or lock and unlock their front door before they can get in their vehicle and drive to work. Those must be really difficult to live with and learn to overcome, particularly when you consider the amount of time one loses to satisfy their habit's needs.

But the habit that I remember my mom couldn't seem to control was humming. I'm not talking about humming an actual song where you could say, 'Oh, I know what that is, I like that song.' No, it was just a nameless, high-pitched, tuneless kind of humming. Like one long note with no pitch kind of a hum. She did this in supermarkets while shopping, in the car, particularly when she was a passenger (this was usually accompanied by a fast flipping back and forth of her purse strap – we're just piling on the annoying habits now), or anyplace else where the quiet was deafening, for her. I guess she just didn't like quiet, except when she was reading. Anywhere else was fair game for humming. At least mom's habit didn't hurt anyone.

My dad's habit, unfortunately, was drinking.

Me & Them

From Knitting
to Romance Novels

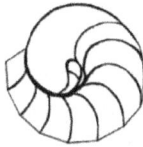

My mom loved to read. Romance novels. I read one, once. I started to read a second one, by the same author, and I thought, didn't I already read this? But not my mom, she couldn't get enough of them. She even occasionally bought one that she already owned and had already read. I wondered how she would know that since the plots were far from varied. But she was a fast reader (I did not inherit that skill) and within a short time would amass a great number of paperbacks. Some of them she passed onto my sister. She also occasionally read a western. She had a strong attraction to the west and westerns – it seems she was always trying to go back to where she came from, despite the poverty and likely abuses she endured as a child.

She also loved to knit. This was mostly a winter hobby. I have memories of her knitting many a pair of mittens, often with the thumb that was twice as long as my own thumb. But they worked fine in their purpose which was keeping my hands warm until, of course, they were so soaked through from making snowballs that it was like wearing two sopping wet dishrags on my hands, which would inevitably begin to turn my fingers numbingly cold.

But the 'piece de resistance' for all of her hard work was the sweater, a gray one with reindeer across the middle and back and additional colors of red and white woven into the scene, that my dad wore until it literally began to fall apart. I remember the holes in the elbows that formed over much time and even more wear. She never did attempt to knit another one, though.

But she did teach me to knit and I would sit next to her, knitting row after row, wondering how I started out with a four-inch row of stitches that somehow grew into a twelve-inch row. To say I was making a scarf would be kind but so inaccurate, unless a scarf is supposed to widen as it is knitted. Not surprising to me, I took up crocheting and have successfully completed several afghans. I did start knitting an afghan but it is still unfinished, tucked away in a closet somewhere.

Me & Them

Visiting Mom

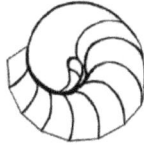

My mom had cancer. We didn't know how much time she had left so my sister, brother, and I made a trip from the east coast to almost the west coast right before Thanksgiving to see my mom and talk to her doctors. She and her husband lived in a small town called Fillmore, the original capital of the state of Utah, which isn't more than a tiny dot on any map, and doesn't exist on others. This would be the last time I saw my mom.

We stayed at the only place in town, The Paradise Inn, fondly referred to as The Parasite Inn by the locals. Since my mom was sick and spent most of the day in bed, we knew we had no choice but to eat our meals out. Of course, our only choice was the lovely greasy-spoon restaurant that was attached to the Paradise Inn. We were tired from our drive, my brother tired from his flight in, and not wanting to search the 1-square mile town to try to find another restaurant, we ate at the Inn.

My husband judges a meal by quantity, I judge by quality. Of course, a bag of Cape Cod potato chips and an Allagash White can occasionally qualify as, if not a quality meal, at least a superior meal over his favorite Utz Barbecue chips and a PBR. We would not have a quality meal at this restaurant and knew it. I, at least, hoped for edible.

So many years have passed since this trip that what I ordered on this one particular day no long resides in my memory. But one item from the meal I will never forget.

The waitress, like so many people we talked to on the trip out there once we reached the mid-west, was friendly. So used to the sometimes rude east coast waiters and waitresses who often treat you like you are imposing on their time and why do they have to wait on you anyway (this seems to occur more in the city than in rural areas) we were grateful and suspicious of the sweet-as-pie attitude that greeted us and took our order.

When the order came, my husband was impressed. Remember, quantity. My sister and I picked, my brother, who has sparingly few taste buds (is this a guy thing?) ate voraciously. A few seconds later the waitress came back with a small bowl of what looked like some kind of whiteish-greenish soup. I knew I hadn't ordered soup as she placed the serving in front of me. I grabbed her before she left.

"Excuse me, what is this?"

"It's coleslaw, hon. It comes with your meal." She was ready to walk away but I wouldn't let her leave as I continued to stare in disbelief at the watery slop that had been placed in front of me.

"No, no, this is not coleslaw."

"It is, hon. That's the way we make it here."

It dawned on me that she was insisting it was coleslaw while my eyes could only see a bowl of vomitus-looking soup. I grabbed the bowl and handing it to her, said as politely and with as little sarcasm as I could inflect in my voice, "No thank you."

Later, at my mom's, the liquid coleslaw mystery was finally solved when I shared my story with my mom.

"The owner of the restaurant, who is also the cook, puts everything in a blender." Yum, I imagined, liquid burgers. I was glad I was no longer eating meat.

Dad

Me & Them

When You Were a Kid

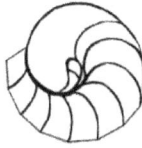

My dad was not much of a talker; at least not to his kids. Whenever we asked him a question, he always had either a sarcastic comment or a witty reply. Seriousness was just not in his makeup, especially when we were kids.

Since my dad's parents came from Lithuania, I thought this made him and his family more interesting since no one knew much about the small country. I had a best friend in the 7th and 8th grades who was 100% Lithuanian. One day, in geography, our teacher was discussing the Baltic states and mentioned 'Lithuania' and someone in class asked, "Where's that?" as if it was a new breed of animal that had just been discovered. My friend and I exchanged glances and smiles. On the plus side, I never heard a joke that started, 'A Lithuanian walked into a bar...'

Lithuanians, to be a Lithuanian or to come from Lithuania, were interesting. That's what I thought. And I was half Lithuanian so I was at least half interesting. Naturally, I wanted to know more about my dad and the country from where his parents had come.

But, it never happened. Our conversations would go something like this:

Me: "Dad, tell me what it was like when you were a kid."

Dad: "When I was a beggarly boy, and lived in a cellar damp, I had not a friend nor a toy, but I had an Aladdin's lamp."

The conversation usually ended there. There might have been a little whining or eye-rolling.

I never did find out much of anything about my dad, his parents, or where they came from. As the quintessential middle child, I believe my dad was lost in the crowd. Throw in a little shyness, a lack of self-esteem, and you have a man certainly not in touch with his feelings, or most likely, anyone else's feelings. But who knows? I could be way off on this. I'll never know.

Me & Them

Please Don't Cook

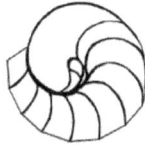

We hated it when our mom was sick. It wasn't very often, but occasionally she would pick up the flu, probably from one of the three of us, and although she sometimes would take a day or so to recuperate, mostly she would just keep going taking care of her children.

When she was too sick to cook, and we were all bouncing back, my dad would step in and cook our Sunday morning breakfast which usually consisted of home fries, fried eggs, and bacon. My dad always got up early and on Sundays he would boil up some potatoes, cut them into good-sized chunks, and let them cook on low in the cast iron skillet with some salt and pepper and a little oil to keep them from sticking. He had mastered this simple dish and we all loved them.

The problem was, the rest of his breakfast was inedible. We begged mom to get up but sometimes she just couldn't do it. We were, after all, only thinking of our own gastrointestinal distress that would surely follow if we had to eat dad's cooking. Dad fried up the bacon until it was a crispy brown. Unlike my mom, he didn't put it on a couple of napkins (paper towels weren't in the budget) to soak up some of the grease. And then, not wanting to dirty more than one pan, the pure yellow, clear, and clean eggs were dropped into the inch of greasy fat like a life raft dumped into a cesspool, absorbing the brown liquid and cooking the egg until the yolk was hard. This blob of grease was put on our plates, now unrecognizable as the egg that came out of the shell, along with the grease-soaked bacon, and perfectly browned home fries.

We would choke down the grease-laden meal, hoping for mom's speedy recovery.

Me & Them

Ethnicity

My dad was first-generation Lithuanian, born of parents who emigrated from Kaunas, Lithuania to the USA. His parents originally landed in Baltimore, MD but somehow ended up in South Boston, MA where they bore and raised their 8 children to adulthood. At the time, South Boston was partitioned off by ethnic groups. This separation led to a branding and you became known by your ethnic group.

I remember hearing my dad talk about his co-workers at the Post Office, "Yeah, this Polish guy…" or "He's an Irish guy…". He was always interested in a person's last name and from there he would figure out what their ethnicity was and most likely where they lived or had grown up. Like his parents, each group found their people and settled close by. I was born and raised outside of Boston, MA and we still had our Chinatown, the Irish in Southie, and the Italians in the North End. The Lithuanians and Polish seemed to be closer to each other, sharing a few favorite dishes. There was the Lithuanian Club that my parents frequented when we were all quite young. Over time his siblings, once out of the military, spread across the state. But they all remained in Massachusetts, a short drive away from each other.

Although there was the identification of a person's background by their ethnic group, I never got the feeling he was saying anything negative about them. It was just a way for him to know a little bit about the person based on where they came from. We all have our negative traits that are passed down to us, along with the positive ones. And some of the seniors who immigrated to our country wanted their son or daughter to marry within their ethnic group. But they also wanted them to be Americans.

It wasn't long before America became known as a melting pot of ethnic groups, as it remains today. In my family, my Lithuanian dad married my part English, part Scotch, and part Dutch mom.

Me & Them

Combs and Pens

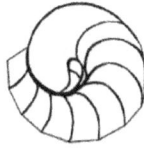

Growing up during the Great Depression created a certain mindset of 'Do Not Waste'. My dad obviously took that to heart. He wouldn't even throw out the fat on beef or pork – these unappetizing morsels would make their way onto his sandwiches.

But there was one habit my dad acquired that, similar to his fondness for half-meat/half-fat sandwiches, always managed to gross us out: he picked up and brought home combs and pens that he found on the street.

Perhaps it was just a by-product of children who lived through the Great Depression to always be looking at the ground for pennies that trained my dad to spot discarded or lost combs or pens. Pens, if they didn't write, were thrown in the trash. Easy decision. Either they wrote or they didn't. My dad loved crossword puzzles and back when the Boston Sunday Globe had a challenging crossword puzzle, my dad would spend some of his free time during the week working on it. Perhaps that was his interest in picking up pens. You never know when one will run out of ink. And refills for cheap pens were not readily available.

Combs can be washed (which, thankfully, he did) and then reused. But again, like the meat/fat sandwiches, just too gross for any of us. I don't think we were lacking for combs in our house but he must have accumulated quite a few over the years.

I also enjoy working on crossword puzzles, but I can honestly say I have never picked up a pen off the street to take home. I buy my pens by the dozen. But I didn't live through the Great Depression, either.

Me & Them

Christmas Tree Shopping

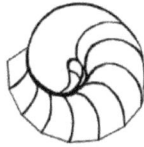

Christmas was two days away and we still didn't have a tree. No artificial trees for us, which in the 1950's only came in silver or a bright pea green that almost looked more artificial than the silver one. From a distance the silver one could sort of pass for ice-covered shiny snow. The farther you got from the green tree the more it stood out from everything else around it whether it was outside in nature or sitting in a stand in the middle of your living room. One of my aunts always had one, complete with the red-brick cardboard fireplace and the scent of evergreen room deodorizer.

But we had to have a real tree with the natural scent of evergreen that could not be duplicated in a spray can. Only this year we didn't have the money. So just two days before Christmas, when the guys selling the trees just wanted to get rid of as many as they could, we went looking for our tree.

My dad had some change in his pocket and was hoping to get a tree for what he had.

"It's almost Christmas eve." Dad tried reasoning with the guy. The lot still had more than a few dozen trees left. The man wanted three dollars for the sadly misshapen tree. Dad wanted to pay a couple of quarters for it.

"There aren't any branches back here." I pointed out, as I walked around the tree, checking it out from all sides, wondering which side would face the living room and which would go against the wall.

"OK," the guy said, "give me 2 bucks." Which was still $1.50 more than my dad had.

Dad walked around, picking up one tree and then another, sighing out loud.

"They don't have anything left. All the trees are bare." Dad said this loud enough, hoping to make his case to drive the price down further. Every tree resembled the first one we picked up. The guy followed us around, picking up one, shaking the snow off it, and when dad walked by, would run ahead to the next one. We were the only ones there – we knew the guy couldn't sell all his trees before Christmas.

"Maybe we should try the other place." Dad turned as if to leave. My brother and I looked at each other. That's it, our looks said, we aren't getting a tree this year.

The guy was getting a little weary – you could tell he had dealt with tough customers since Thanksgiving when the trees had first arrived. And with just one day left to sell as many as he could, at 9:10pm, he just wanted to go home.

He threw his hands up and said, "OK, mister, name your price. I just wanna go home."

Dad fished in his pocket and took out the two quarters. "I've got two bits."

"OK, here ya go. Merry Christmas."

Dad took the tree the man handed to him and with my brother grabbing the top, they carried it to the car where my mom and sister were waiting.

"Merry Christmas." I waved a soggy mitten at the man, trying to suppress a smile. We had our tree.

Me & Them

Dad Making Chips

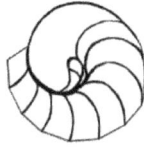

Thinking back to my childhood, I do remember dad making a few special foods. They weren't your usual steak and mashed potatoes. The preparation of those food items were reserved for mom. Dad's were more rare, and they all seemed to involve the same main ingredient: grease. Grease or oil or some kind of lard, whatever dad cooked, if it were made today, would be a heart attack waiting to happen. Deep frying was his favorite kind of cooking; donuts, French fries (peeled potatoes and cut like steak fries), and potato chips, sliced thin. And they were all delicious.

All of the fried items he made were put into paper bags in a half-hearted attempt to soak up some of the grease. Donuts were put into another paper bag with cinnamon or powdered sugar. The French fries and chips were, naturally, put into bags that had salt in them and then shaken gently. The paper bag would turn from a tan color into a nearly translucent sepia. All of these items were eaten warm, when they tasted the best.

To this day, potato chips are my favorite. And the more they taste like home-made the better.

Me & Them

Romanian Easter Eggs

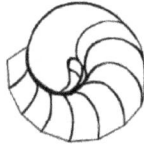

When my dad first started working at the Post Office, he was focused on learning his new job. He'd spent hours, before he got the job, studying for the test. I'm not sure but I have a feeling it isn't as difficult to pass the postal exam as it once was. He was on the night shift so we had to be quiet when we got home from school because he was sleeping. He worked this shift for a few years until he accumulated some seniority.

It was during this time that one day he came home with two beautiful Romanian Easter eggs. I had never heard of them before but I remember we were all in awe of the deep purple colors that we could never achieve with the Easter egg coloring kits my mom bought. Some people stick a pin hole in the egg and drain the liquid. The ones my dad bought from the Romanian woman were solid.

My dad was inspired. Not much into any kind of arts or crafts, he took to Romanian Easter eggs like Monet to haystacks. The apartment we lived in at the time had a section of the stovetop that was flat where, at Christmas, dad would, after boiling them first, roast chestnuts. It was also great for melting the beeswax, an item he had on hand from when he worked in the tailoring business, used in the egg decorating process.

After boiling the eggs, dad would take one and with the head of a common pin dipped in the melted beeswax, he would begin creating his design on the pure white egg shell. He used the Romanian eggs as a model for his design and would spend hours with the one egg. Then he would dip the egg into one of the colors. By then we had all completed coloring the rest of the two dozen eggs complete with some kind of design; a bunny or a chick or maybe just our name, written with the wax crayon that was provided in the kit.

For several years my dad tried to duplicate the intricate lace-like design the Romanian woman had created on her eggs but he never came close. I'm sure she spent many more hours than just the couple my dad spent each Easter.

We kept the Romanian eggs for years in a china closet that was in my parents' bedroom. Over the years I would shake them and you could hear the light bump of the egg inside that had shrunk down to a small ball. I don't think they survived our move from the apartment we had lived in for eight years because I never saw them again after that.

Me & Them

Cigarettes and a Pipe

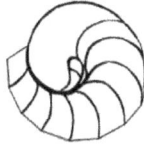

I grew up a smoker – not that I actually smoked when I was a child, but I was exposed to smoke from both of my parents. My mom was a casual smoker, lighting up a Camel while enjoying a cup of coffee. She quit when I was in my early teens. My dad was a die-hard smoker. His smoking not only affected him, but his family as well.

But there was one time when his smoking could have been fatal, to both him and me. My dad, a drinker as well as a smoker, would come home from the barroom, lie on the couch watching TV and fall asleep with a cigarette burning in his hand. After burning holes in the cushions on our couch so many times my mom would flip the cushions, choosing the side with the least number of holes to sit on. Since a new couch was not in the budget, we just had to ignore the burn holes.

On one particular night my mom and sister wanted to go to the movies. Since doing anything sociable did not interest my dad, he stayed home. This night, which was like any other night where you would find my brother studying in his room, was a little different. This night would be remembered in my family as the night my dad could have burned down the house with me and him in it. (I have no doubt my brother would have saved himself.)

I fell asleep on the foot of my parents' bed where my dad was doing crossword puzzles. He fell asleep also, with a cigarette in his hand. The next thing I knew my mom and sister were yelling and taking me out of the room while shaking my dad awake. He had fallen asleep and the cigarette was smoldering through the mattress. They had only been gone about an hour; the movie they wanted to see wasn't playing so they decided to come home.

Mom and dad bought a new mattress.

Not long after this dad took up the pipe, a less dangerous alternative if only because it took more concentration to hold the bowl and puff. It certainly improved the smell in the house because while cigarettes seem to suck up the air in the house, the cherry tobacco smoke, although as harmful as cigarettes I'm sure, was much preferred by all of us. But it was a temporary change – smoking cigarettes in the post office where dad worked was convenient whereas smoking a pipe was not. So he mostly smoked the pipe at home and continued to smoke cigarettes at work.

It didn't really matter which he smoked at home because we were all breathing in the second-hand smoke.

Me & Them

A Parent-Teacher Talk

<table>
<tr><td colspan="2">A = Best work</td><td colspan="2">D = Not passible; Privileged to attend Summer Review School.</td></tr>
</table>

		A = Best work	FULL CREDIT	D = Not passible; Privileged to attend Summer Review School.	NO CREDIT		
		B = Good work		E = Very poor. Must repeat year's work.			
		C = Passible work					

SCHOOL YEAR 19 6 3 19 6 4	Sept. Oct.	Nov. Dec.	Jan. Feb.	Mar. April	May June	Year's Record
Days Absent	O	O	O	O	O	O
Times Tardy	A	A	A	A	A	A
Conduct						
Effort	A	A	A	B	B	A B
English (7-8-9)	B	B-	B	B	A	B
Math (7-8)	B+	A-	B+	B-	A	B
Basic Math (7-8)						
Algebra I (9)						
General Business (9)						
History (7-8)	B-	B	B	A	A	B
Geography (7-8)	B-	C+	B	B+	B	B
Ancient History (9) FRENCH	A-	B	B	A-	A-	A
Fine Arts (7-8-9)						
H. Ec. (7-8-9)						
Foods						
Clothing						
Applied Arts						
Ind. Arts (7-8-9) Ind. Arts or Ex. Ec. (7-8-9)	A	C	C+	B	B	D
Mechanical Draw. (9)						
Gen. Sci. (7-8-9)	B	B	B	B	B	A B
Math - Gen. Science	B	B	B	B	B	B
Art (7-8-9)	B	B	B	B	B+	B
Art Appreciation (9)						
Civic Ed. (9)						
Physical Education						A B
Health Education (7)	B-	B	B	B	B+	B
Guidance (8-9)						
Penmanship (7-8)						
* Foreign Language						

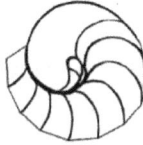

Who doesn't love a parent-teacher conference? Students, mostly, unless they are straight-A students, which I was not. But sometimes parents also do not look forward to this school ritual. My mom was the designated parent who met with our teachers. Occasionally my dad had to go if my mom had other plans that night.

The one time I can remember my dad going to a parent-teacher meeting for me was when I was in the 7th grade. I can say (without knowing absolutely for sure) that he did not go to talk to all of my teachers, but I do know for sure that he did talk to one of my teachers and that is the one I got a report back on. He talked to my geography teacher.

I remember asking my dad about this teacher and what he said about me. I'm not sure my dad even mentioned me to this teacher, I'll call him Mr. Baronowski. My dad was always really interested in a person's ethnicity and would try to figure out what nationality they were when he heard their last name. He often identified people by their nationality saying things like 'Yeah, he's an Irish guy' or 'a good Polish family'. Back in the 1950's people were, more often than not, only one nationality. Identifying a person by their nationality apparently told you something about the person, if you believed in stereotypes. But today's families are more likely to be of mixed nationality and people really can't be identified in this same way.

But I know that this is at least partially what my dad talked about with my geography teacher, Mr. Baronowski. Not about me; they talked about where on the map they each hailed from. My dad and my geography teacher. They talked about geography.

Me & Them

Working at the Post Office

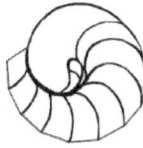

My dad was a tailor. He worked on men's overcoats. A piecework job, he didn't make a salary but got paid by the number of pieces he finished each day. Since overcoats were made during the summer months for the coming fall and winter season, his most profitable months were during the summer season. And then when the winter months came, which included Christmas, work was slow and he sometimes had to sign up for unemployment. Until he took a test at the Post Office.

I remember the months that he studied. Diligent in his determination to pass this test, he spent many hours preparing for the test that would change his career path. And then he took the test – and passed. A new job when he was in his mid-to-late 30's, he started at the bottom and was given the least attractive hours – the graveyard shift. I remember coming home from school in the afternoon and was told to be quiet because dad was sleeping. And then he left for work when it was almost time for us to go to bed, coming home the next morning when we were leaving for school.

Back before the post office was automated as it is today, each clerk had to learn his 'scheme'. A scheme consisted of a series of streets in several neighborhoods covering a lot of towns. He devised his own system for memorizing that started with a small 3"x5" binder with lined paper. And having a knack for memorization, or a mnemonic that helped you remember, was key. My husband's friend, Darren, is a doctor. He commented that 'anyone can do' what he did to become a doctor. What he was good at was memorization as in body parts and what they did and how they were connected and most of all, the technical name for each. He had to have the mental aptitude to have so many medical terms at his fingertips. But my dad applied his ability to remember to streets and towns that were part of his scheme.

I remember dad spending hours studying his notebook, making side notes, learning the streets and towns that were his responsibility to memorize. And then sometimes he would hand his precious notebook to one of us and ask us to name a street and he would tell us the town it was in. We tested his knowledge and he passed with flying colors. His memory served him well through all the years he worked at the Post Office.

Me & Them

Crossword Puzzles and
Other Hobbies

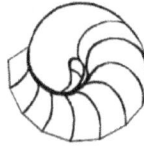

It seems most people have some kind of a hobby. Sometimes it is collecting things, like stamps, coins, shoes, nutcrackers, or any number of other mostly irrelevant items. Or they may take up painting, drawing, or learning to play the piano. But we take up these other interests almost as a distraction to what we do in our day job. And then, for some, a hobby becomes a life-long passion and they give up their day job to pursue painting or writing as a full-time career.

My dad had a couple of hobbies, one of which was taken up mostly because of its connection to his day job working at the post office. He was a philatelist, as they're called, or a stamp collector. It was a natural progression since he looked at letters from not just all over the USA but all over the world that came to the Postal Annex in South Boston, MA. I do remember buying him a single stamp one year that I, of course, wrapped in a box that a sweater could fit in. The stamp cost me $15. Not a huge price but that was in the 1970's – adjusted for today's prices that would be about $100.

Years later after my dad passed, we were at a family get-together and I overheard my mom tell a relative that I always wanted my dad's stamp collection and she was giving them to me. I piped up, no I don't, I don't care about the stamps. "Fine," my mom said, "I'll give them to someone else." My nephew got them. I know, stupid. I was in college at the time, in my late 20's, and strongly embracing and fine tuning my sarcasm. How many things in life would we love to do over?

But my dad's most favorite hobby and one that he continued to his dying day was crossword puzzles. The Boston Sunday Globe used to have one that was more challenging than a lot of others. My dad would look up words, mulling over the answers, working on the puzzle in his free time throughout the week, knowing a new puzzle was coming on Sunday. And he worked on it until it was completed. Of course, this helped us all with Christmas gifts – a book of crossword and other challenging puzzles was always a welcome gift. I have the last jumbo crossword puzzle book that I bought for my dad. Only a few of the puzzles are completed. But there are also lots of drawings here and there throughout the book. Maybe this was something that at one point was another interest for my dad that he never pursued. My sister and I both draw and paint and my brother, when he was a teen, created many funny caricatures.

Also, like my dad, I enjoy and have many jumbo crossword puzzle books. Sometimes we are more like our parents than we think.

Me & Them

Personal Hygiene or Not

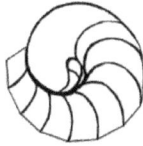

I often wondered what attracted my mom and dad to each other. Like most meetings I believe it was being in the right place at the right time; and, at that time, there was enough of an attraction to lead them to the altar and marriage. My dad, if I had to guess (and I do) was a bit shy. My mom, I knew for sure, was insecure. A match made in heaven (I say this with tongue-in-cheek).

And then they had three kids together. And life goes on.

Over the years, as often happens, they gained some weight, my mom more than my dad. No one worked out at a gym in the 1950's, or could afford it, unless you lived near a YMCA, which we didn't. Mom, of course, was lifting babies, doing laundry, vacuuming the house, cooking, shopping, ironing, etc. so was getting a good amount of exercise. It wasn't until we got a little older and no longer needed to be carried or chased around the house that my mom put on a few pounds, which was easy when you're 5'1" tall (so I've been told). My dad walked – that was his main form of exercise. He never drove a car; he either walked or took the subway wherever he needed to go. We always lived close enough to either a train station or a bus stop. When my dad worked at the post office the train took him right to downtown where he worked at the South Boston Postal Annex.

So, as they both aged, besides the weight gain and all of the other joys that come with aging, and after so many years together in marital bliss (again, tongue-in-cheek), we saw the personal hygiene start to drop off. Funny, though, I never saw it with my mom. She always smelled like Jergens hand lotion or when she was going out, White Shoulders perfume. A little mascara, rouge, and a splash of that Coty lipstick, that as a child I liked so much, and she was ready to go out. This, of course, was all after she took a bath or a shower and took the pin curlers out of her hair. My dad, on the opposite side of the spectrum, would run a comb through his hair (he had a countless number of combs) put on his shoes, wearing whatever clothes he was hanging out in around the house, and he was ready to go. No shaving, no after shave, I'm not even sure he washed his face or brushed his teeth. And I'm being generous when I say he ran a comb through his hair. Sometimes I think running his hand through his hair could easily substitute for a comb (even though he had so many combs).

And then more than once, and when I say more than once I mean at least half of the time, unless they were going to a wedding, my dad was smelling of stale smoke and beer that clung to his clothes from his nightly visit to the barroom on his way home from work. So, Jergens hand lotion and perfume vs. stale smoke and beer. I guess you really have to love someone.

Me & Them

The Thief

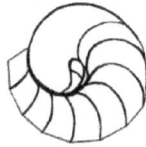

He waited until she was in the bathroom, showering. Or when she was hanging laundry outside on the clothesline. Or maybe involved in one of her favorite movies, a western. Like a cat burglar moving silently, avoiding the places on the floor that he knew creaked when stepped on, he opened the bedroom door and peeking inside, stepped over the threshold and into the space that held the treasure he was seeking. He scanned the room; the bed, the nightstand, her side, the high bureau, and then he spotted it, on the far side of the dresser, there it was, in plain sight: the purse.

Walking as lightly as he could with her acute hearing just on the other side of the door, he headed for the one ticket out of the house. At least for an hour or two. And it was there, in the purse. He unsnapped the top, pausing as he reached inside, and slowly and with deft fingers, pulled the wallet out. Quickly now, he opened it, reaching into the dollar bill section, and pulled out 2 or 3 ones. There were only 3 more left and nothing larger. It was a risk but he had to take it. He needed to take it. He had no other choice. He put the wallet back into the purse and snapped it shut. Wait, was it snapped shut? He couldn't remember, but he decided to snap it and just hoped she wouldn't remember either.

Backing out of the room, checking the hallway to be sure he was completely undetected in his crime, he stepped gingerly over the threshold once more, pulling the bedroom door shut behind him. He walked as quickly and quietly as possible on the old linoleum floors to the back door and, unlatching the chain and turning the knob, he opened the door, stepped out into the back hallway, and closed the door behind him. Without looking back.

Me & Them

The Barroom

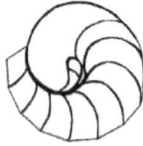

In the 1950's there were plenty of pubs or bistros where men and women hung out together and had a drink or two. But this wasn't the type of place my dad frequented. I knew my dad's favorite hangout was a place my mom never went. As a matter of fact, very possibly back then when there were strict rules about where a woman belonged in society, they may have been banned from going inside where my dad spent a lot of his time. That place was called the barroom.

Friday nights were often dinner at a favorite restaurant and a trip to the drive-in. After dinner we stopped at the local 5-and-10 cent store where, with just a nickel, we each bought what we wanted. My sister and brother often bought candy. I was fascinated by, and still can't resist, the rainbow pads of paper. And then we were off to the drive-in that had a playground with swings and a slide for kids before the movie started. Then once it did start and we were back in the car within a matter of minutes I was asleep.

Dad did not leave the barroom willingly. I wondered if he told his 'friends' there that he even had a family. But beeping outside the bar never got a response so my mom would send my brother inside to get him. I remember one time I asked to go. A little afraid of this dark, windowless place that my dad seemed to prefer to my mom or us, his children, I had to see what was the appeal.

When I walked through the door with my brother, I looked around expecting to see at least bright colors and fun activities. But all we were greeted by was a stale-beer smelling, smoke-filled room with a long bar where men stood or sat on stools. The rest of the room was mostly empty except for a few tables where a few other men sat talking, a tankard of beer in front of each of them. My dad turned and, finishing up his beer, escorted us out the door. The other men smiled, watching us walk away. I wondered if they, too, had wives and kids at home.

I never asked to go in the barroom again. The mystery of it was over for me. The only mystery that still remained was why my dad preferred the barroom to his home with his family.

Me & Them

The Man of the House

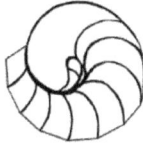

The sound of vomiting always turned my stomach. It was my dad, sick from drinking too much alcohol. It wasn't until much later that he figured out he could drink beer all night without the hangover effects that mixed drinks gave him.

My two older siblings, Rita and Steve, and I would run out the back door to the porch, out of earshot of the retching sounds coming from the bathroom. A small apartment, there really wasn't any place else we could go where the sound would not reach us. Even in winter, without coats, the fresh, cold air filled our lungs with a cleanliness that erased the sound that often lingered in our ears for hours later. We laughed, unsure of what dad's alcoholism really meant to us, or understood the effect it had on all of us, individually. Only much later would we come to know these things.

And then, per mom's instructions, one or all of us would walk to the corner store for ice cream. Always vanilla, dad's favorite. It seemed something cold and sweet helped with his hangover. Hours later he would emerge from the bedroom looking bedraggled with the sour smell of losing the entire contents of his stomach trailing behind him. We would gag, reflexively and almost in unison, for we were sure we had escaped the rancid odor along with the distressing sounds of vomiting while out on the back porch.

My dad wasn't the man I hoped he would be, unlike some of my friends' dads. The good dads were interested in my friends, took them for ice cream or to ball games, made a point of talking to them and showing interest in their interests and schoolwork. My dad didn't drive but instead walked or took the subway everywhere. And he didn't seem interested in much but watching ball games on TV, working at his job at the post office, going to the barroom, and doing crossword puzzles. Mom was the disciplinarian, the cook, the cleaner, the one we went to for everything. Sometimes it was as if dad didn't live there, or didn't even exist in the house. His presence, whether physically there or not, was hardly noticed. Only years later and after much therapy did I understand how much his drinking took away from our family, from each and every one of us.

On Saturdays he would slip out of the house. Most of the family was involved in their own activities. It wasn't until hours later that mom would ask, 'Did you see your father?' We didn't know he had left the house, thought he was watching TV or talking to a neighbor while sweeping the sidewalk. That was often how he planned his escape. If any one of us did notice him leaving through the back door he would take the broom and sweep the sidewalk at the front of the house. He seemed to enjoy gossiping and I imagine the neighbors thought he was the nicest guy.

But we all knew his destination, really, was the barroom. That was his plan all along.

Sundays were different. No barrooms were open so he was stuck, like a caged animal, indoors with his family. Again, we all went our separate ways. I mostly went outdoors to play with my friends in the neighborhood. My sister stayed in her room listening to the record player, fixing her hair in different styles, applying makeup. My brother, the smart one, was either studying in his room or went out with his friends. We all had chores but the small apartment never took much time to clean. My mom had cooking to do; Sunday was usually a big dinner day. The roast beef or hamburger-stuffed pork roast in the oven filled the apartment with the warm smells of a home-cooked meal. Deboning the pork roast was a chore only my dad would attempt. He liked busy work, something he could focus on so he wouldn't have to think about anything else in his life. Like meditating. Or praying. After that the TV was his to watch whatever sport was taking place during that season. I sometimes wondered if my parents had bought a home, and there were always things to take care of, if he might not have run off to the barroom but instead got involved in projects around the house. When my sister and brother both married and we visited each of them at their homes, my dad could be found raking in the back yard. This was his sidewalk sweeping activity that was like his Yoga. Alone, in his own thoughts, with no interruptions, he was focused.

But we were told that he didn't want to buy a house. When my dad's parents both passed away, the money they had (they had bought two houses – and these were people who emigrated from Lithuania to Boston, MA) was divided among their children. Several of my dad's brothers used their money to buy homes. If I had to guess I would say my dad drank his share away.

Me & Them

No Dogs Allowed

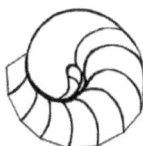

It was time to move again. I was starting high school so they chose a town they were familiar with near a high school that I could attend. It was a large apartment with enough rooms so we could each have our own bedroom. My brother was in college and my sister was on the verge of getting married. There was only one problem: no pets. We had a small dog, a mutt, a fox terrier mix, that we'd had for several years after having gotten her when she was just a few months old. There was no other way, we had to bring her to the pound. And my dad was the one to do it.

He was gone several hours. I remember how upsetting it was for all of us having spent so many years with the little dog we called Mickey. We got her for free; she was little and wiggly and I fell in love immediately. A spontaneous decision, we had nothing for her the day we brought her home; no bowl for food, no bed to sleep in, no toys for playing. She was our first dog.

She was in her prime and still had many years left in her the day my dad brought her to the pound. It was too long ago so I don't remember all the details of the day. What I do remember, though, is the most important detail and nothing else matters: my dad showed up back home several hours later, with

Mickey. He said, "Forget it, we're taking her with us. She's a little dog, she won't be any trouble. We'll just move in and it will be months before they even see her and by then, well, we aren't moving." We were all so excited to have Mickey back with us.

She was my playmate the first few years; we were, after all, both children. As she grew up into an adult dog, she accompanied my sister on many walks. And as she aged and we all moved on and out of the house, she became my mom's companion. She had a good long life with us. Thanks to my dad.

Me & Them

The Homebody

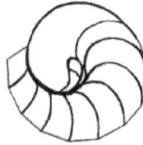

Despite my dad's addiction to drinking and spending a lot of his free time at the barroom, he was a homebody. Not only did he not want to visit anyone, he also didn't want anyone to visit him. They were an unlikely couple, mom and dad, since my mom loved to visit people, loved having company, and loved traveling.

So occasionally my mom would get her way and they would travel. With the exception of the one time we took a trip to visit my mom's relatives out west when I was eight, we, as a family, never took a vacation. In the summer we would take a Sunday and, with many of the other relatives, would meet at a lake that we would all drive to and hang out for the day. I have some fond memories of the days we spent at this lake. But a week's vacation? Never.

Once we were all grown and out of the house, it must have been more and more difficult for my dad to say 'no' to my mom, who was itching to get behind the wheel of the car and drive for miles to somewhere, anywhere, USA. Anywhere beyond the few relatives she would visit regularly; sisters-in-law and her best friend, mostly. With both of them working there was no excuse like the one we heard regularly during our childhood, 'We can't afford it.' They needed gas for the car, a couple of hotel stays, and money for food. There was not an excuse that could stick – he had to give in and travel or mom would have taken off by herself, I have no doubt.

One trip they took that I can recall was to visit my mom's brother in North Carolina. Not more than a couple of days to drive there, they visited with my uncle, his wife, and their two children who were also grown and out of the house but came to visit their aunt and uncle from Massachusetts. North Carolina has many places to visit and if my mom, again, had her way, they were on the go for the entire week.

I can imagine my dad, before they left, trying to manufacture some excuse as to why he couldn't go. He had accumulated so much vacation time at this point that he could have taken 3 months off with pay and still have more vacation time available. But again, they never went on vacation. Most people use up their vacation time in a year and start borrowing against the next year. Not my dad – he could have sold some of his vacation time to his fellow employees and made a little money. I wonder if that was legal?

But when they returned, that was when the homebody turned into world-wide traveler. That was all he could talk about for weeks on end. He collected rocks from places they went (this was a particular hobby of my mom's that my dad seemed to share, too – they were, after all, free items that you could just pick up off the ground), he showed the photos of the gardens they walked through and all the wonderful experiences they, well, experienced. You would think he had never been on a vacation before. And he hadn't.

Me & Them

On His Way Out

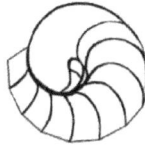

"How are you feeling today, dad?"

"Good!" Said with a little too much enthusiasm. He's
lying. I knew he was lying, he knew he was lying. But
these things were not talked about. We wanted
everything to be rosy and bright. We wanted to live
the lie. We had to. We were afraid of the truth, even
though it stared us all right in the face. The house
smelled of bleach and laundry detergent, as if the
entire place had been cleaned, floor to ceiling, with the
disinfectants. That sickening-sweet smell of Mountain
Breeze or Floral Spring. I kept the door to my
bedroom closed. I burned patchouli incense. At night
I locked my door.

It was the sheets. They needed to be washed daily.
There were fluids, I think. I didn't ask. Something
that oozed out. Perhaps it was inner decay. All I
knew for sure was that he was dying. We all knew.
From the inside out. It was a slow death. But that
was his plan. He never meant to live a long, healthy,
and happy life. It was pre-planned. Everything he did
was a step in the right direction. Or wrong direction,
depending on your plan. But this was his plan. And
we all watched. And waited.

We knew for sure when we all met at mom and dad's apartment for Thanksgiving. Dad was a shell of a man, his clothes seemed two sizes too big. His face, once bloated from too much alcohol, now had the appearance of a skeleton with sunken cheeks and a thin parchment layer of skin. His bones were more prominent. Everywhere. When he sat his kneecaps stood out from his pant legs. His elbows appeared as daggers out of the arms of his shirt.

Mom was tired but put on a cheerful face as she served the turkey dinner. We all posed for a photo - our last together. We smiled, we turned away. It was as if we were each posing for a portrait photo. We talked, we laughed, we joked. Then Steve talked to dad. You need to see a doctor. You're sick. Mind your own business. "I tried," Steve said.

I happened to be living with them at that time. I was getting my degree, getting divorced, and I had a new lover. Things were complicated. My responsibilities were invisible to some, real to me. One more thing and then one more thing and then another. I put my energy into my lover. I studied, we studied, we went to school, we made love, we studied. I stayed with my parents more than I wanted. The sickening sweet smell of laundry. It came to smell only of death to me.

"How are you doing, dad?"

"Ok." He stayed in bed, always. His frail, shrinking body walked, his feet found the way, to the bathroom. Sometimes he came down the hall, toward my bedroom. His sense of direction had been eaten by the disease. I checked my lock, my stomach shaking. He was an invader in our home. Gone the man who paid our bills, worked to feed us, watched TV, read the Sunday paper, carved the turkey, made coffee, deboned the pork shoulder, stopped every night at the barroom. Gone the father who drank too much, smoked too much, swept the sidewalk, chatted with the neighbors, and never showed a single loving moment to his children. Unless you count the time he took us out, on Christmas Eve, to get a Christmas tree for fifty cents, or the many times we all walked to the beach to dig for clams, or the time he took our only dog to the pound because the apartment owner said we couldn't have a dog, and then he brought her back home and we still got the apartment.

He had a lot of sick days from work. He took them all. He had insurance with his job. He never used it. None of us did. We called a doctor who made a house call. He needs to go to the hospital. Dad said "No." We called an ambulance. He said 'no' again. Mom was exhausted. She slept on the couch now. She woke when he woke. She cleaned him. She fed him. She changed his sheets.

He was heading for the bathroom - I heard him fall. In my bed, I listened, frozen with fear. Mom came to help him.

"You have to help me - I can't lift him." He lay on the floor, looking like the outline from a crime scene. Pale and bone thin. I didn't want to touch him. Will I catch it, I wondered for just a second? I was being unreasonable in an unreasonable situation. We got him up, like lifting a bag of building blocks, hard and chunky. She got him back to bed. We didn't sleep, we cried.

"He has to go to the hospital." I was searching for assistance. I didn't find any from those I called. My lover came to my rescue. We wrapped him in a blanket, we carried him down the stairs and put him in the car. The hospital brought him to another hospital for veterans. They told us what we already knew. Cancer. He was quiet, the man made of popsicle sticks. His eyes never looked so blue. Bloated from liquor for years, I never noticed. They cleaned him up. They changed his sheets. They fed him.

I tried to study. It was summer - warm and comfortable, I needed to study. My lover kept loving me. I failed my class. And then, at 59, he died.

Me & Them

Stranger at the Wake

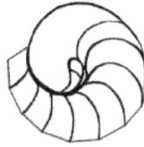

After about a year of seeing dad deteriorate while the cancer spread through his body, he passed away on Father's Day. Just a little ironic since he was not a model dad. It was more like he was a non-dad. My brother has some fond memories of going to a couple of baseball games and throwing the ball with dad. I have no such memories.

We went through the usual motions; setting up wake and funeral times, purchasing a casket, and contacting relatives. We did what needed to be done and took our places next to our mom at the wake. Condolences were given by relatives and a few friends.

And then this man showed up. It was June and hot. The man, who was probably in his early 50's, was conservatively and appropriately dressed in a short-sleeved dress shirt and pants, and a tie. He didn't stay long but stopped to speak to my mom. Although it was so many years ago and I don't remember exactly what the man said, I will never forget the impact his words had on our family.

Taking my mom's hands in his, he told her how sorry he was for her loss. And then he talked about my dad like he was the best friend anyone could have, and how special he was, and how lucky he was to have known him. He told my mom these things as if she already knew it and shared the same sentiments about my dad.

And then he left.

We looked from one to the other, our mouths agape. This stranger spoke about a man none of us knew.

"He was at the wrong wake," my brother said; and we each echoed the sentiment, laughing about the man's obvious confusion. But if he wasn't, and I'm quite sure he said my dad's name when he greeted my mom, there is a part of me that was jealous of this stranger who knew my dad in a way that I never did or ever would.

Sometime later we went through dad's things. Among his sparse belongings that he felt were worth keeping, we found a few postcards that dad had received while working at the post office that were addressed to him at the post office. They were from exotic places, the kind of places my dad would never see in his lifetime. They were signed 'Stan'. I remembered the stranger who came to dad's wake and thought that on the day of dad's wake, we met Stan.

Image Credits

"Doctor's Bag" by Santa Cruz Museum of Art and History is licensed with CC BY 4.0. Desaturated from original.

To view a copy of this license, visit http://creativecommons.org/licenses/by/4.0/

> *Doctors, Dentists, and*
> *Other Unnecessary Professions* – page 11

Green Stamps Booklet
Sperry and Hutchinson Company (Publisher)

> *Green Stamps* – page 33

"Roasted Turkey" by kimberlykv is licensed with CC BY 2.0. Desaturated from original.

To view a copy of this license, visit https://creativecommons.org/licenses/by/2.0/

> *Favorite Foods* – page 49

Cowboys of Southern Colorado. 1930. Desaturated crop from original.
https://ark.digitalcommonwealth.org/ark:/50959/w3 763k63z

> *Westerns* – page 59

About the Author

DJ Geribo is the author of several children's books, a non-fiction book, and a collection of short stories. Living in rural New Hampshire with her husband, two Pomeranians, and a Cockatoo, the author finds inspiration surrounded by nature and the frequent wildlife visitors that come by. "Me & Them" is DJ's sixth book.

DJ is always working on new books and you can find out about her upcoming releases by visiting her website at: https://www.djgeribo.com

All of DJ's books can be purchased from her website and they can also be purchased directly from the publisher at www.BBDPublishing.com.

Selected titles are also available on Amazon in both softcover and Kindle e-book formats.

www.ingramcontent.com/pod-product-compliance
Lightning Source LLC
Chambersburg PA
CBHW031124020426
42333CB00012B/220